Pocket Room
Coloring Book

Thank you for purchasing our book! We hope you enjoy it and find it useful. If you have a moment, we would love it if you could leave a review so that other readers can hear your thoughts on the book. Thanks again and have a great day!

9 798323 388035